Ted & Paul

Down On The Farm

Keith Godwin

Copyright © 2022 Keith Godwin

All rights reserved.

ISBN: 9798416306892

DEDICATION

In memory of my cousin Jean who I shared many summers with and created wonderful memories of the holidays we spent together over the years.

My thanks again go to Kelly East without her, these Ted and Paul stories would not be published.

Thanks also to my friends Mervyn and Marian Thomas for their help with the several Welsh words that appear in the story and congratulations to former pupil Tommy Price for being a part of this Ted and Paul story.

CONTENTS

	Acknowledgments	i
1	The Chance Of A Holiday	1
2	The Journey Begins	7
3	Aunty Gwyneth	21
4	Off To Market	29
5	The Old Gentleman	46
6	Trouble For Ted	65

FOREWORD

Welcome to this, the third book in the Ted and Paul series. In this story our two heroes are invited to spend a week's holiday with Clarissa and her parents on their farm in North Wales.

We are introduced to Aunty Gwyneth, (Clarissa's mother) and her bone crushing hugs, Uncle Idwal (Clarissa's father) and Sidney, the not always obedient sheepdog.

The boys have a busy time on the farm, taking sheep to market, helping milk the cows and cleaning out the cow shed.

Ted has a close encounter with a bull. They save a boy from drowning in the canal and Ted gets into trouble with the police.

Just the sort of things you would expect in a Ted and Paul story!

BACKGROUND

I was a teacher at Cwmcarn Primary School in the beautiful Welsh Valleys for 36 years. I taught pupils from 1972 to 2008. During my early years there, I started telling my class stories that I had written about 'Ted & Paul.'

The stories came in handy time and time again as the children would always know that if they weren't on their best behaviour, I would not be reading them pages from my Ted & Paul stories at the end of the school day.

Over the years, I ended up writing seven stories altogether, enough to last the whole of the school year. Throughout the 36 years I taught at Cwmcarn Primary, I must have read them to well over a thousand of my pupils.

Whenever I meet any of those pupils today, they always ask the same question, "When are you going to publish your Ted & Paul stories Sir?" They've had a long wait, but now, thanks to Kelly they are at last being published.

My former pupils at Cwmcarn may have forgotten much of what I taught them, but they certainly have not forgotten the Ted & Paul stories.

I hope they will get as much enjoyment reading them now, as they did when they first heard me reading them in my class all those years ago.

Ted & Paul – Down On The Farm was originally written in September 1978. 43 years later, it has finally been published!

CHAPTER 1

The Chance of a Holiday.

Clarissa had been spending a couple of weeks with her cousins Ted and Paul at their home in South Wales. The boys had been dreading her visit and at the start of it, Clarissa had caused them more than a few problems but as time went on things improved and by the end of the two weeks, Clarissa had been made a member of the Grizzly Gang and had helped redecorate Sleepy Hollow, Mrs. Muldoon's old house.

It was the day before Clarissa was due to go home. The day was wet, and the three children were forced to stay indoors. This did not please Mr. Thomas. He was trying to watch the television, but the children kept wandering in front of the screen, much to his annoyance.

"Ted, will you get out of the way!" shouted his father, "I'm trying to watch the television."
"Sorry," apologised Ted as he scuttled out of the way.

No sooner had Ted moved out of the way than Paul wandered in front of the screen.

"Paul!" yelled his father, "get out of the way!" With a mumbled apology, Paul darted out of his father's way only to be replaced a few minutes later by Clarissa cradling her doll in her arms. Before he could shout at her, the phone in the hall rang.

"I'll get it," he called out to his wife, "I might as well, I can't watch the television in peace with these three cluttering up the house."

He went out into the hall and picked up the receiver.
"Is that Llanfyllech 2069?" asked a voice on the other end of the line.
"It is," replied Mr. Thomas.
"Are you sure that's Llnfyllech 2069?" asked the voice.
"Of course I'm sure," answered Mr. Thomas, "I live here."
"Who's that speaking?" asked the voice.
"This is Mr. Thomas," replied Mr. Thomas.
"Oh, it's you is it," said the voice.
"Of course it's me. I just said it was me," snapped Mr. Thomas, beginning to get irritated with the voice at the other end of the line. "Who's calling?" he asked.
"Me," replied the voice.

"Who's me?" he asked.
"You're Mr. Thomas," answered the voice, "Don't you know who you are?"
"Of course I know who I am," shouted Mr. Thomas. "Who are you?"
"This is Gwyneth here," said the voice, "Is Gladys there?"
"I should have guessed," thought Mr. Thomas. "Hold on Gwyneth I'll get her for you."

He went out to the kitchen where his wife was busy baking.
"Your sister is on the phone," he told her.
Mrs. Thomas wiped her hands on her apron and hurried to see what her sister wanted.

"Hello Gwyneth. How are you? Nothing wrong I hope"

Mr. Thomas returned to the front room hoping to watch the racing on television without further interruptions.

"Who was on the phone, Dad?" asked Paul.
"Your Aunty Gwyneth," he told him.
"Mum?" said Clarissa, "I wonder what she wants?"
"No idea," said her uncle, "I'm sure we'll all find out when your aunty finishes talking to her."

It wasn't until a half hour later that Mrs. Thomas finished her conversation with her sister and came into the front room.

"Well?" asked her husband "What did Gwyneth have to say that took half an hour?"
"Not a lot," replied his wife.
"Not a lot?" repeated her husband." You were on that phone for half an hour. I'm glad I wasn't paying for that call."
"She just rang to check the details for tomorrow when Clarissa goes home," she told him.
"And is everything arranged?" asked her husband.
"Yes," replied his wife. "Her father will pick her up at midday tomorrow."
"Good," said Mr. Thomas, settling down to watch the television.
"She also asked if the boys would like to go back with her and spend a week with them on the farm." she added.
"Of course they'd like to," said her husband with a huge smile on his face. "I think that's an excellent idea. I'll be able to watch television in peace and our stairs will have a week's holiday from these two elephants charging up and down them."

From the look on the boys' faces, they did not think it was such a good idea.

"But dad..." began Ted.
"No buts," said his father, "you're going to spend a lovely week with your Uncle Idwal, Aunty Gwyneth and Clarissa on the farm. Just think of all that fresh country air and all the fun you'll have working on the farm."

Clarissa was very excited at the thought of her cousins staying with her. She'd had such a good time while she was staying with them she was glad she'd have their company for another week.

Ted and Paul looked miserably at each other. They did not want to go. It was bad enough when Aunty Gwyneth came to visit for a day but at least she went home at the end of the day. Now they would be stuck with her for a whole week. It's not that Aunty Gwyneth was unkind to them, in fact just the opposite. She always made such a fuss of them with endless hugs and kisses. They both hated that! Then there were all those early mornings. Farmers always got up early and there was all the work to do round the farm they would be expected to help out with.

"So you think we should let them go?" asked his wife.
"Of course!" he replied. "They'll have a wonderful

time!"
"And I'm going to have a wonderful time while they're away," he thought to himself.
"You'd better go and pack the things you're going to need," their mother told them.
"I'm glad you're coming to the farm," said Clarissa as she went with them to help them pack.

The boys were far from happy with the idea of spending a week on the farm.
The only people pleased with the arrangement were Clarissa and of course, Mr. and Mrs. Thomas.

Chapter 2

The Journey Begins.

The following morning at half-past eleven, a rather battered old Land Rover pulled up outside the house and out got Uncle Idwal and a black and white sheepdog. They came up the path and were met at the front door by Mr. and Mrs. Thomas. The moment they came into the house, the trouble began. Uncle Idwal's dog spotted Ted's cat!

"Look out!" warned Ted.

The warning came too late, the animals spotted each other, and the cat shot into the kitchen with the dog in hot pursuit. Ted made a dive for the dog but missed.

"Oh, dear," groaned Mrs. Thomas.
"Come here Sidney," Uncle Idwal called out to the dog.
"Sidney?" said Paul, "Who on earth's Sidney?"
"That's what dad calls his dog," Clarissa told him.
"What a daft name for a dog," thought Ted as he got up off the floor.

The children, followed by the adults ran into the kitchen where they found the dog chasing the cat round the kitchen table.
"Heel, Sidney!" commanded Uncle Idwal.

The dog took no notice and continued to chase the cat.
"I thought sheep dogs were supposed to be obedient and obey their masters." muttered Mr. Thomas, making a dive for the cat and missing.

"Butterfingers!" said Ted.

Mr. Thomas glared at his son as the cat shot out of the kitchen and up the stairs closely followed by Sidney and the three children. He groaned as he heard the three children thundering up the stairs.

"Not only have I got elephants charging up my stairs, but I've also got a cat and dog as well!" he groaned.
"Elephants?" asked a puzzled Uncle Idwal, "I haven't seen any elephants."

By now the children had reached the boys' bedroom into which the animals had disappeared. Inside, they found the cat had taken

refuge on top of the wardrobe while Sidney was leaping up at it barking madly. Clarissa grabbed Sidney's collar and took him downstairs while Ted rescued a very frightened cat.
"I think we'd better be going," announced Uncle Idwal.
"So do I!" thought Mr. Thomas.
"Thank you for having Clarissa," he added, "I hope she hasn't been too much trouble."
"No trouble at all," Mrs. Thomas told him. "We've enjoyed having her."
"Make sure you behave yourselves," Mr. Thomas warned his sons.
"We always do," Ted replied
"Don't stand any nonsense from them," Mr. Thomas told his brother-in-law.
"Don't worry," laughed Uncle Idwal, "There's plenty of work to do on the farm to keep them out of mischief."

The boys did not like the sound of that, and Mr. Thomas did not believe it was possible for his sons to stay out of trouble however busy they were kept!

The children carried their cases out to the Land Rover.

"Clarissa and I will travel in the front," Uncle Idwal told the boys. "You, Sidney and the luggage will have to travel in the back."
He opened the back door of the Land Rover, and the boys went to climb in.

"'Pooh!!" gasped Ted, "There's a terrible smell in here!"
"Nothing to worry about," their uncle informed him.. "I had some pigs in there yesterday."
"It's all right for him, he's sitting in the front!" complained Ted.
"I suppose we should be thankful the pigs are not still in here," said Paul.
"It smells as if they still are in here," said Ted. "We could be gassed to death by the time we get to the farm!"

Mr. and Mrs. Thomas stood on the front doorstep waving until the Land Rover disappeared from sight.

"Well!" said Mr. Thomas, "A whole week of peace and quiet!"
"I can't remember the last time we had the house to ourselves," said his wife.
"It's going to be like heaven," sighed her husband as they walked back into the house, closing the

front door behind them.

The Land Rover soon left the village far behind as it made its journey north to Brynhyfryd Farm. The journey seemed endless especially for the boys in the back of the vehicle. Not only did it smell bad but the wooden side benches they sat on were very uncomfortable.
After what seemed like hours the Land Rover came to a halt in a lay-by at the top of a hill. Uncle Idwal and Clarissa got out, walked to the back, and opened the door.

"Fresh air!" gasped Ted, taking a deep breath.
"Have we arrived?" asked Paul.
"No," replied Clarissa. "We've got a puncture."
"Oh no!" groaned Paul, "We'll never get there at this rate."
"You'll have to get out while I change the wheel," their uncle told them.
The boys were glad to get out and stretch their legs.
"Get the spare out of the back, boys," their uncle told them.
"OK," said Ted, lifting out the spare wheel while Paul held on to Sidney's collar to stop him getting out.
"Oh, uncle," Ted called out.

"What is it?" he asked.
"It's the spare wheel," replied Ted it's flat!"
Uncle Idwal began muttering to himself in Welsh as he handed Paul the foot pump.

"You pump it up while I get the other wheel off." he told him.

Jacking up the Land Rover he began to remove the wheel while the children took it in turns with the foot pump to inflate the spare one. After a few minutes Paul stopped pumping.

"Why have you stopped?" asked Ted.
"I'm feeling a bit TYRED," chuckled Paul.
"I'm not in the mood for your jokes." Ted told him.
"You take over and WHEEL soon get the job done," added Paul with a huge grin on his face.
"I'm warning you!" threatened his brother.

It was taking Uncle Idwal longer than he expected to remove the punctured wheel and as the children had finished pumping up the spare one, Ted and Paul were amusing themselves by rolling it back and forth between them.

"I'm ready for the spare now," their uncle called out.

Ted turned to his uncle just as Paul rolled it towards him.

"Ted!" Paul yelled out a warning.

The warning came too late, and the wheel shot past Ted heading for the top of the hill on which they were parked.

"Runaway wheel!" yelled Ted, as he and Paul chased after it.
"It's getting away," yelled Paul.
"I'm not blind!" snapped Ted.

The wheel reached the top of the hill and disappeared down it. Once it began rolling down the hill there was no way the boys could catch up with it. They watched in dismay as the wheel, gathering speed, headed for the bottom of the hill. The only good thing was there was no traffic on the road, or it might have caused an accident. The wheel
was fast approaching a road junction at the bottom of the hill.

"I hope nothing is coming along that other road," puffed Ted as they raced on down the hill.

Luckily there was no other traffic about but the watched in horror as the wheel hit a kerb at the junction, flew into the air and disappeared over a hedge and into a field. They reached the hedge, gasping for breath and peered over it looking for the wheel. There it was floating on a pond in the field with a duck sitting on it.

"Who's going to get it?" asked Ted.
"You are." his brother told him.
"Why me?" complained Ted.
"Because you're the one who let it escape." Paul replied.
"But I'm going to get wet," moaned Ted.
"If you ask that duck nicely, perhaps she'll push it over to you." chuckled Paul.
"Very funny," said Ted as he climbed over the gate and into the field.

Neither of the boys had noticed that something in the field would mean the pond was going to be the least of Ted's problems. At the far end of the field, out of sight from the boys a very large bull was grazing.
Ted stood at the edge of the pond looking at the wheel with the duck sitting on it.

"Get on with it," called Paul from the other side of

the hedge.
"I suppose I'll have to go for a paddle," complained Ted.

Sitting on the edge of the pond, he took off his shoes and socks and rolled up his trouser legs. Standing up he slowly waded into the pond. The water was freezing, and Ted could feel the mud at the bottom of the pond oozing between his toes. He reached the wheel expecting the duck to dive off it and swim away, but it just sat there watching him.

"What am I going to do?" asked Ted. "It won't move."
"Ask it nicely and it might," suggested his brother.
"I am not talking to a duck!" Ted yelled back. "People will think I'm quackers,"
"Get on with it," shouted Paul impatiently.
"Shoo!" Ted shouted at the duck "That's a good idea," called out Paul. "Throw your shoe at it. That'll shift it!"

Ted glared at his brother and reached out to push the duck off the wheel. The duck pecked at him catching him on his fingers.

"Ouch!" yelled Ted, holding his fingers.

"What's the matter now?" asked Paul.
"This killer duck has just attacked me." Ted informed him.
"Don't tell me you're afraid of a little ducky wucky?" Paul asked him.
"This little ducky wucky has nearly pecked the tops of my fingers off!" shouted Ted.

Getting more and more annoyed with the killer duck, Ted grabbed the wheel and shook it violently. It did the trick. Quacking her annoyance, the duck jumped off the wheel and swam away.

Ted grabbed the wheel and began wading with it towards the edge of the pond. As he did so, Paul spotted the bull which had appeared from behind some trees and was slowly walking towards the pond.

"I think you'd better get a move on," advised Paul.
"Don't tell me the killer duck is sneaking up on me?" said Ted.
"It's a bit more than a duck," Paul told him.
"Don't tell me it's two ducks!" said Ted.

By now the bull had reached the edge of the pond and stood observing the boy standing in it.

"I don't know how to tell you this," said Paul.
"Tell me what?" asked Ted.
"You'd better look behind you," suggested Paul.

Ted slowly turned round and saw the bull. He almost fell over with the shock.

"I want my mummy!" he wailed.
"Don't panic," Paul told him.
"That's easy for you to say from where you are," said Ted
"Perhaps you can come out on this side," suggested Paul.

Ted slowly began wading towards the side furthest away from the bull. Unfortunately, the bull began walking to the side Ted was making for.

"No good," warned Paul, "it's coming round to head you off!"
"I'm trapped!" wailed Ted, "What am I going to do?"
"I'll go and get Uncle Idwal," Paul told him.
"Don't leave me!" moaned Ted. "It may come in to get me."
"What are we going to do then?" asked Paul,
"I don't know, said Ted, "Can't you think of

something?"
"Have you ever thought about becoming a bullfighter?" suggested Paul.
"If you can't think of anything sensible, don't bother," snapped Ted.
"Only trying to be helpful," said Paul. "You could have used your red shirt as a cape."
"Red shirt!" gasped Ted. "Oh no! Bulls are supposed to charge at anything coloured red!"
"I'll see if I can distract him," said Paul.
"Do it! Do it!" yelled Ted.
"Here bully, bully, bully." called out Paul.
"'You idiot!" Ted told his brother, "He'll think you are mad."
"What if it's mad?" suggested Paul.
"What do you mean?" asked Ted.
"Perhaps it's got mad cow disease." his brother replied.
"Well thank you very much," said Ted. "That's all I need, trapped in a pond by a crazy cow!"
"Bull," Paul corrected him.

The bull settled itself down on the grass at the edge of the pond from where it continued to watch Ted.

'Oh, look!" said Paul, "It's Sitting Bull." using the name of the North American Indian chief who defeated General Custer and the Seventh Cavalry at the Battle of the Little Bighorn in 1876.

"Very funny!" said Ted, not at all amused.
"Try getting out on the opposite side," suggested Paul.

Ted began wading to the side furthest away from the bull.

"Has it moved?" he asked his brother.
"No," replied Paul, "I think it's gone to sleep."
"Are you sure?" asked Ted.
"Yep!" said Paul. "Looks like a BULLDOZER to me."
"I'll kill him!" threatened Ted.

The bull made no attempt to move as Ted waded out of the pond and rolled the wheel towards the gate. Then he began edging round the pond to collect his shoes and socks.
They were a lot closer to the bull and it watched him as he got nearer.

"There's a nice bully," crooned Ted, "let your Uncle Ted get his shoes and socks."

On the other side of the gate, Paul held his

breath as his brother stooped to pick up his shoes and socks. With them safely in his hands, Ted began slowly backing up towards the gate. Paul had already collected the wheel and Ted scrambled over the gate to join his brother.

"I thought I was a gonner there," he told his brother as he put his socks and shoes back on. "Let's get this wheel back to Uncle Idwal," said Paul. "He'll be wondering what's happened to us."

They trudged back up the hill where they found their uncle and Clarissa waiting for them.
"What took you so long?" he asked them."
"Ted had to fight a duck to get the wheel back." Paul told him.
"Fight a duck?" Clarissa asked.
"Ignore him," said Ted, glaring at his brother, "He's trying to be funny."

With the wheel back on the Land Rover, they continued on their way north to the farm. The rest of the journey was uneventful but because of the puncture they were late arriving. It had already started to get dark as the land rover pulled off the main road and began the climb up the narrow lane which led to Brynhyfryd Farm.

Chapter 3

Aunty Gwyneth

The Land Rover came to a stop in the farmyard and the boys climbed out of the back carrying their suitcases. Looking towards the farmhouse they could see their aunty standing by the front door,

"Yoo-hoo!" yelled out Aunty Gwyneth as she began running towards them.
"Look out!" warned Paul, "Here she comes!"
"I hope she doesn't want to kiss us." replied Ted.
"Hello, my lovely boys!" screeched Aunty Gwyneth, "Come and give your aunty a great big kiss,"
"I was afraid of that," whispered Paul.
"I suppose we'd better kiss her," whispered back Ted,
"Come on, don't be shy, I won't bite you," laughed their aunty.
"I should hope not," thought Ted, as he walked towards her "It'll be bad enough having a kiss."
"My word, what a big boy you're getting," she told him.

Before he knew what was happening, his aunty

made a grab for him. Not only did he get a kiss from her, but he also got a hug as well.

Now Aunty Gwyneth's hugs were not like your normal aunty's hugs. Her hugs were more like the hugs you would receive if a grizzly bear took a liking to you. Ted thought she was going to break his back! When she finally released him, he staggered back to rejoin his brother.

"Blimey!" he groaned, "It's like being hugged by a bear!"

Paul had no time to reply as his aunty grabbed him and proceeded to welcome him in the same way she had welcomed Ted. When he too was released by her, he staggered back to Ted.

"Nothing like being hugged by a bear," he told him. "More like by a gorilla!"

"Come on boys," called out their aunty, ""suppers on the table."
"Supper?" said Ted, looking at his watch, "It's only seven o'clock,"
"She must mean tea," replied Paul as they walked into the farmhouse.

The boys put down their cases and sat at the kitchen table, eager to tuck into their meal.

"You'll have to wash your hands first," Clarissa informed them. "Mam thinks it's very important to wash your hands before you have a meal."
"Very sensible," agreed Paul, "especially after our adventures with the spare wheel."
"Where's the bathroom?" asked Ted.
"Bathroom?" shrieked his aunty, "We haven't got one of those. Use the kitchen sink like we do."
"OK, aunty," said Ted.

The boys walked over to the kitchen sink. First they looked at the sink and then they looked at each other. They'd never seen a sink like this one. It didn't have any taps!

"Where are the taps?" whispered Paul.
"Well I haven't got them!" whispered back Ted.
"What's the matter boys?" Aunty Gwyneth called over to them, "lost the soap?"
" No," called back Ted, "just the taps."
"Taps?" shrieked Aunty Gwyneth, "We don't have any of those!"
"Use some water from the bucket under the sink," Clarissa told them.
"What a funny house," said Ted as they washed

their hands with water taken from the bucket under the sink.
They dried their hands on a towel, Ted remarking that at least they had towels, and went to join Clarissa at the table, she having already washed her hands. Aunty Gwyneth placed their meals on the table.

"Wow!" exclaimed Paul on seeing the size of it.
"We always have big meals," Clarissa told him.
"Perhaps it won't be too bad here," thought Ted who was already tucking into his meal.

When they had eaten until they could eat no more, Aunty Gwyneth and Clarissa cleared away the plates. The Boys didn't offer to help because they didn't think they would be able to move after eating so much.

"That was a fantastic meal, aunty," said Paul.
"Yes," agreed Ted, "I think I will just be able to sit and watch television as long as I don't have to move too far to get to the set."
"Television?" shrieked his aunty, "We haven't got one of those!"
"What's on the radio then?" asked Paul.
"Oh...." began Clarissa.
"Don't tell me," interrupted Ted, "you haven't got

one of those."
"Oh yes we have," Clarissa told him indignantly.
"Thank goodness for that." said Paul, "At least we'll be able to listen to some music. I wonder what's on?"
"Nothing", Clarissa told him.
"There must be something on," said Ted, "it's only half past seven."
"There's nothing on," insisted Clarissa.
"How do you know?" asked Paul.
"Because our radio is broken," she told him.
"Oh great!" groaned Ted. "No taps, no tele, no radio! Some holiday this is going to be!"

Aunty Gwyneth came back into the room.

"Do you want to go to the smithfield with your uncle tomorrow?" she asked her nephews.
"What's so special about Mr. Smith's field?" asked Ted.
"I should think one field looks much the same as any other field." added Paul.
"Not Mr. Smith's field," laughed Clarissa, "the smithfield."
"What's a smithfield?" asked Ted.
"It's a place where farmers go when they want to sell some of their animals." explained his cousin. "Dad is going there to sell some of his sheep."

:"That sounds like good fun," said Paul.
"Then you'd better get off to bed and have an early night," their aunty told them. "You'll have to be up early in the morning."
"Bed?" whispered Ted to his brother, "It's too early to go to bed!"
"We might as well," whispered back Paul, There's nothing else to do."
"That's true," agreed Ted. "Goodnight aunty."

The boys picked up their suitcases and made their way to the stairs to go up to their bedroom.

"Just a minute boys, haven't you forgotten something?" their aunty called after them.
"No, we've got our suitcases," Ted informed her.
"Don't tell me you're going to bed without kissing your aunty goodnight," she scolded them.
"Sorry, aunty, we forgot," apologised Ted.

He walked across to his aunty with a worried look on his face, anxious to get the ordeal over and done with. Paul watched him go knowing only too well it would be his turn next.
The kiss as kisses go wasn't too bad but the hug was a different matter. It felt like she was trying to squeeze him to death. Once he was released, he stepped back to allow Paul to take his place.

Once his ordeal was over Clarissa showed them the way to their bedroom.
"She almost smothered me that time," complained Paul as they climbed the stairs.
"Your mother doesn't know her own strength." Ted told his cousin.
"She does get a bit carried away," agreed Clarissa.
"It's us that'll get carried away," said Paul, "On stretchers if she keeps hugging us like that!"
"Are you coming with us tomorrow?" asked Ted
"Of course," said Clarissa, "See you in the morning."

The boys unpacked their cases and got ready for bed.

"Oh, my aching back," groaned Ted as he lay down on the bed."
"She'd make a good all-in wrestler," said Paul.
"Well I wouldn't take her on," Ted told him,
"I'm looking forward to tomorrow," said Paul.
"We'll be like cowboys on a cattle drive like you see in western films."
"Except we're taking sheep not cows," Ted pointed out. "I suppose we could call ourselves sheep boys instead of cowboys, but it doesn't sound so good,

The boys settled down and were soon fast asleep. The long journey from their home to North Wales had tired them more than they realised

Chapter 4

Off to Market

The boys were awakened the next morning by a dreadful noise coming from the yard below their window.

"What on earth's that?" asked Paul sitting up in bed and yawning.
"Sounds like someone being strangled," said Ted.
"Perhaps it's some poor unfortunate visitor being hugged to death by Aunty Gwyneth," chuckled Paul.

There was a knock at the door and Clarissa came into the room.

"I see Colin has already woken you up," she said.
"I haven't seen any Colin," said Ted. "Who's Colin?
"All we've heard is an awful noise out in the yard," said Paul.
"That was Colin," laughed Clarissa. "He's our rooster. He always wakes us up in the mornings."
"I think I'd prefer an alarm clock," muttered Paul.
"Yes," agreed Ted, "At least you can turn an alarm clock off."
"Is it time to get up?" asked Paul.

"It certainly is," Clarissa told him, "it's seven o'clock."
"It's far too early," complained Ted. "It's still dark outside."
"If you don't get up you'll miss your breakfasts," she warned them.
"We're getting up, we're getting up," yelled Ted, leaping out of bed.
"We'll be down in a couple of minutes," said Paul as Clarissa left the room.
"We're going to need another holiday to get over this one." complained Ted.

The threat of missing breakfast had done the trick. The boys hated missing their meals. In three minutes they were downstairs, sitting at the table waiting to be served.

"You've forgotten to wash," their aunty told them. "No breakfast until you have."

They rushed over to the sink without taps, got some water from the bucket underneath it and had the quickest wash in history.
"My that was quick" commented their aunty as the boys began tucking into their breakfasts.
"Where's Clarissa?" asked Ted, speaking with a mouth full of food.

"Don't speak with your mouth full," his aunty scolded him.
"Sorry, aunty," apologised Ted, swallowing his food.
"She's helping her father load the sheep into the lorry." She explained.

Aunty Gwyneth left the boys to finish their breakfasts. It was just as well she had as they were shovelling food into their mouths so fast she would certainly have told them off for eating so quickly if she had seen them. By the time she came back they had finished and were ready to leave.

"On with your coats and off you go." she told them.

The boys made their way to the door.

"Haven't you forgotten something?" their aunty called after them.

By now, the boys knew exactly what that meant. They hadn't kissed her goodbye and received their daily dose of torture from her hugs. They made their way back to their aunty and each in turn received a goodbye hug and kiss.

"Have a good time," she called after them as they staggered out of the kitchen.
"My back is not going to stand much more of this treatment," complained Ted as they made their way across the farmyard to where a cattle lorry was parked.

At the back of the lorry, Uncle Idwal and Clarissa were busy herding sheep up the ramp and into the lorry.

"Bore da, boys," Uncle Idwal greeted his nephews.
"Why would I want to borrow your dad?" Ted asked his cousin.
"Dad's saying good morning to you in Welsh," she explained.
"Borrow dad," the boys replied to their uncle.
"I hope we don't have to learn Welsh while we're here," thought Ted.

At that moment, two of the sheep broke away from the others and wandered off into the farmyard.

"Bring them back boys," their uncle told them.

Ted and Paul set off in pursuit of the sheep.

There followed an entertaining five minutes as Uncle Idwal and Clarissa watched Ted and Paul attempting to round up the wayward sheep. Each time they thought they had them, the sheep managed to get away. At last, they managed to trap them in a corner of the yard.

"Got you!" announced Ted, confidently.

Unfortunately, his confidence was misplaced, and the sheep jumped over some boxes and escaped again.

"Oh, look," said Paul as the two sheep leapt to freedom, "a couple of wooly jumpers!"
Ted glared at his brother, "That's not helping" he growled.

Uncle Idwal thought it was time he gave the boys some help. At a whistle from him, Sidney began herding the two sheep back towards the lorry. The boys watched as they scampered up the ramp to join the others.

"Why didn't he do that in the first place?" asked Ted.
"Sidney's a lot better with sheep than he is with cats," commented Paul, remembering how the

dog had chased their cat.
"I just hope we don't have to travel in the back with the sheep." said Ted.

Ted and Paul were pleased to find out they did not have to travel in the back with the sheep. They were not so pleased however when Paul found he had to have Clarissa sitting on his lap and Ted ended up with Sidney on his.

"I don't like having Clarissa on my lap,' whispered Paul.
"Stop complaining," whispered back Ted. "At least she doesn't keep licking your face."

Sidney had taken a liking to Ted and was continually licking him. It reminded Ted of Dilys, Mrs. Muldoon's donkey who used to do the same thing.

The journey was terrible, the lorry seemed to find every bump and pothole in the road. To help pass the time, the boys took turns in trying to pronounce the names of the villages they passed through. They failed miserably much to Clarissa's and their uncle's amusement.

"How on earth do people pronounce the names

of these places?" asked Ted.
"It's easy," Clarissa told him and proceeded to name the next two villages they passed through.
"Think yourselves lucky we're not going to Anglesey," their uncle told them.
"Why's that, uncle?" asked Paul.
"There's a village there which has a very long name," he replied.
"What's it called?" asked Ted.
"You tell them Clarissa," said her father.
"It's called "Llanfairpwllgwyngyllgogerychwyrndrobwllllantysiliogogogoch,"
she told them.
(Author's note: Good luck with the pronunciation of that!!)

Ted and Paul sat open-mouthed as their cousin recited the name.

"You've got to be joking," said Ted as she reached the end of the name.
"That's easy for you to say," Paul told his cousin.
"Just think if you lived there and someone asked you where you lived!" said Ted.
"It would be even worse if you had to write it down.," added his brother.
"Imagine getting that in you'd weekly spelling

test in school," chuckled Ted.
"The people who live there shorten it to Llanfair PG." their uncle explained as he steered the lorry into the smithfield market and stopped next to some animal pens.

"Give me a hand to unload the sheep and get them into the pen and then you've got until 3 o'clock to do what you want," Uncle Idwal told them.

They all made their way to the back of the lorry where uncle Idwal unlocked and lowered the ramp. Ted expected the sheep to trot obediently down it and into the pen. Ted unfortunately didn't know much about sheep and that they rarely did what you wanted them to do. The sheep remained where they were watching him.

"Ted, you'll have to go up the ramp and drive them out." his uncle told him.
"OK, uncle," said Ted, and began walking up the ramp.
"Mint sauce, mint sauce," he chanted at the sheep.
"What on earth are you doing?" asked Clarissa.
"Scaring them out," explained Ted. "You put mint sauce on lamb when you have it for dinner,"

It wasn't the mint sauce that scared the sheep into moving. Ted slipped on the ramp and went crashing down on it. This delighted Paul and Clarissa, but the noise scared the sheep into action, and they began running down the ramp towards Ted who lay directly in their path.

"Help!" yelled Ted, "Mad sheep!"
"Keep your head down," advised Paul as the sheep thundered towards his brother.

Once the first sheep began to move, the rest followed. Some went round Ted, others jumped over him, but a few ran right over him. At the bottom of the ramp, Uncle Idwal herded them safely into the pen and closed and bolted the gate behind them. Paul and Clarissa ran up the ramp and helped a rather dazed to his feet.

"Are you all right Ted," asked a concerned Clarissa.
"I think I'll live," he replied, brushing himself down.
"He doesn't look too baaaaad," bleated Paul.

Ted glared at his brother, not at all amused.

"Are Ewe all right?" chuckled his brother.
"You wouldn't find it so funny if it had happened

to you," Ted told him.

"Oh look." said Clarissa." pointing to a man approaching them. It's Uncle Mervyn."

"Bore da Mervyn." Uncle Idwal greeted him.
"Bore da Idwal." replied Mervyn. "I see you've got two new helpers."
"They're my two nephews from South Wales." he explained to his friend.
"Mervyn and his wife Marian own the farm next to mine." he told the boys.

Mervyn shook hands with the boys, each of them grimacing with pain as Mervyn gripped their hands.

"Now we've got crushed hands as well as crushed backs to worry about." Ted whispered to his brother.

Uncle Idwal took Ted to get him cleaned up and when this was done he gave each of the children some money to spend and reminded them to be back by 3 o'clock. He and Mervyn went off to talk to some other farmers and the children made their way into the town. First of all they bought an ice cream each and sat on a seat by the canal to eat them while trying to decide what they were going to do,

"Clarissa, you know the town," said Ted, "Where can we go?"
"We could visit the castle," she suggested, "it's a mile outside the town."
"That's a long way," replied Ted, not impressed with her suggestion.
"We could walk through the park and look at the deer," she told them.
"The dear what?" asked Paul.
"The deer the animal you idiot," giggled Clarissa.
"Oh," laughed Paul, "Silly me!"
"Or we could go to the cinema and watch a film." she told them.
"Now that's a good idea," said Ted. "How do we get there?"
"Follow me," she told them and set off along the towpath with her cousins.
"Are there any fish in the canal?" asked Paul.
"I don't think so," replied Clarissa.
"Well he won't have much luck," replied her cousin, pointing to a young boy fishing from the canal bank.
"Caught anything?" asked Ted as they walked by.
"Not yet" replied the boy.

They walked on along the towpath towards the lock. They were looking down into it when they heard a scream and a splash. Looking back along the towpath they saw the part where the boy had been fishing had collapsed and the boy was now splashing frantically in the dark water of the canal.

"Quick!" yelled Ted.

The three children dashed back along the towpath until they reached the part that had collapsed. Ted tried to grab the boy, but he was just out of reach.

"What are we going to do? What are we going to do?" wailed Clarissa, beginning to panic.
"Let me dive in," said Paul. "I can swim."
"It's not safe," warned Ted, " You might get caught in the reeds."
"What are we going to do? What are we going to do?" wailed Clarissa, continuing to panic.
"Give me your belt, Paul," said his brother.
"But my trousers will fall down," protested Paul.
"Never mind that!" snapped Ted. "Quick, or that boy is going to drown."
"It's all right for you," complained Paul, "it's not your trousers that are going to fall down."

Muttering to himself, Paul undid his belt, took it off and handed it to his brother.

"What are you going to do with it?" asked Clarissa.
"I'm going to use the belt as a lifeline," explained Ted. "I'll hold on to one end and throw the other end to him. It should reach."

Ted made a loop at one end of the belt and holding on to the other end threw it to the boy. Luckily it reached him on the first attempt, and he held on grimly as Ted slowly pulled him towards the bank. Clarissa held on to Ted with both hands while Paul held on to her with one hand while his other hand held on to his trousers to prevent them ending up round his ankles! With some difficulty they managed to pull the boy out of the canal and onto the towpath.
It was then they found out the boy had stopped breathing.

"Clarissa, run to the telephone kiosk we passed and ring for an ambulance." he ordered. "I'll try and revive him."

Clarissa shot off like a rocket towards the kiosk and Ted began to try and revive the boy using artificial respiration which he'd learned about at his first aid class. He didn't know if it would work. He'd practiced on a dummy, but this was a real person. He desperately hoped it would work, Clarissa in the meantime had reached the kiosk and dialled 999.

"Emergency. Which service do you require?" asked a voice on the other end of the line.
"Ambulance please," panted Clarissa.

There was a pause, then another voice came on the line.

"Ambulance service, What is the nature of your emergency?"
"A boy has fallen in the canal," she explained. "We've managed to get him out, but he's stopped breathing."
"Do you know how to revive him?" asked the voice.
"My cousin is trying to do that now." Clarissa replied.
"Good!" said the voice. "Now tell me exactly where you are."
"I'm in a telephone kiosk," replied Clarissa.
"No," said the voice patiently, "What I should have asked is where is the boy."

"He's on the canal towpath just below the lock." said Clarissa.
"Got it," said the voice, "I'm dispatching an ambulance now."

Clarissa hung up the phone and ran back to her cousins. Ted had managed to get the boy breathing again but he was still unconscious. In the distance they could hear the siren of the approaching ambulance. A few moments later it turned down the lane to the canal and came to a halt alongside them. Two ambulance men got out and hurried across to them. They examined the boy who was beginning to come round.

I think he's going to be OK," said the one.
"Who gave the artificial respiration?" asked the other.
"I did," said Ted.
"What's artificial perspiration?" asked Clarissa.
"It's respiration not perspiration," Paul informed her. "It's what you use to revive someone when they've stopped breathing."
"Well done, son," the ambulance man congratulated Ted. " You saved this boy's life."

The boy was gently placed on a stretcher and carried to the ambulance. One of the men stayed with the boy while the other came back to ask Ted a few questions.

"What's your name, son," he asked him.
"Ted Thomas," replied Ted.
"And where do you live?" he asked.
"I live in South Wales." said Ted, "but I'm staying at Brynhyfryd Farm with my cousin for a week."

The man wrote the details down in his notebook and returned to the ambulance. The children watched as it reversed up the lane and disappeared from sight.

"That was exciting," announced Paul.
"Here's your belt." said Ted, "Put in on before your trousers fall down, That would prove much too exciting for us."
Clarissa started giggling.
"They've nearly come down twice already," Paul informed them as he put his belt back on.
"Come on," said Clarissa, "Let's get to the cinema or we'll miss the film."

They made their way along the towpath, over the footbridge and into the town and were soon standing outside the cinema looking at the notice board to see what film was being shown. It was a western which pleased the two boys but not Clarissa. They made their way up the steps and into the cinema.

Chapter 5

The Old Gentleman

Once inside the cinema the children joined the queue of people waiting to buy tickets. Soon the three of them reached the front of the queue.

"Three tickets please," Ted said to the lady behind the counter.
"Upstairs or downstairs?" she asked him.
"Just a minute please," replied Ted turning to the other two. "Do we want to go upstairs or downstairs?" he asked them.
"Ask her how much the tickets are," Paul told him.
"How much are the tickets?" asked Ted, turning back to the lady.
"Upstairs or downstairs?" she repeated.
"Just a minute, please," said Ted turning once again to the other two. "Do you want to know how much it is upstairs or how much it is downstairs?" he asked them.
"Both, you fool," replied Paul. "Then we'll know if we can afford to go upstairs or not."
"How much is it upstairs and downstairs?" Ted asked her.

While this had been going on, an elderly

gentleman had joined the queue and was getting rather annoyed at being kept waiting by the children in front of him.

"Hurry up!" he snapped at Ted. "I want to see the film!"
"All right all right, "Keep your hair on," replied Ted rudely.

Not only was it rude of Ted, but it was also impossible for the man to keep his hair on as he was bald!

"Why you cheeky young....." began the man.
"Three upstairs, please," said Paul quickly, hoping they had enough money to pay for the tickets.

Luckily they did so they bought their tickets and left the queue.

"About time," said the man as they walked away. "Can I have one adult and one child downstairs please," he asked the lady behind the counter.

"Bad tempered old so and so," muttered Ted.
"Come on," said Paul, "before you get us into trouble."
"Who does he think he is?" continued Ted angrily.

"Come on," insisted Clarissa, "or we're going to miss the start of the film."
"Just a minute," said Ted," I want to buy a drink."

He turned and hurried over to the refreshment kiosk. Unfortunately, he was not looking where he was going, and he bumped into the man from the queue.

"Sorry," he apologised, at first not realising who he had collided with.
"You again!" shouted the man. "Why don't you look where you are going,"
"I said I was sorry," snapped back Ted.

The old man glared at Ted and stormed off into the downstairs section of the cinema with the little girl who was with him. Ted bought his drink and hurried back to Clarissa and his brother.

"Why don't you look where you're going," Paul told him.
"Don't you start," said Ted, "I've already had that from old misery guts."

They made their way upstairs and got to their seats just as the lights went out. They were lucky to get three seats in the front row which gave them a good view of the screen. They settled down in their seats and after taking a sip of his drink, Ted placed it on the ledge in front of him.

The first film was a cartoon which they all enjoyed. The main film was a western with battles between the cowboys and the Indians. Ted was thoroughly enjoying the film and he was helping the cowboys fight the Indians by shooting at them with an imaginary gun each time one of them appeared on the screen.. The Indian chief appeared on the screen.

"Do you think that's chief Sitting Bull?" Paul asked him, reminding Ted of his encounter with the bull in the field.
Ted ignored him and leaning forward took careful aim at the chief. His hand brushed against his drink on the ledge, and he watched in horror as it fell into the downstairs part of the cinema. There was a yell from the seats below.

"What was that?" asked Paul.
"I think it's time we left," said Ted standing up.
"The film hasn't finished yet," Clarissa pointed out.
"Let's go," said Ted anxiously.
"Aren't you enjoying the film?" she asked him.
"Yes, it's great," said Ted. "Let's get out of here!"

"If you're enjoying it why do you want to leave?" asked his brother.
"Because." hissed Ted, "I've just knocked my drink off the ledge and judging by that shout, someone has just had a shower of orange squash!'
"Time to go then," agreed Paul.

They began walking up the aisle, but they had left it too late. A torch shone on them, and they were taken to the manager's office.

"Which one of you threw orange squash over the balcony?" demanded the manager as they entered.
"It was an accident," Ted told him. " I didn't throw it over the balcony, I knocked it off the ledge.
"It was an accident," Paul confirmed.
"He didn't mean to do it," added Clarissa.
"A likely story!" boomed a voice behind them.

They spun round and found themselves facing the very angry and soggy old gentleman.

"Oh no!" thought Ted, "Why did it have to be him?"
"This boy has caused nothing but trouble since he came into this cinema," he told the manager.

"I think he should be thrown out!"
"Now just a minute....." began Ted.
"Be quiet!" snapped the man. "What's your name, boy?" he demanded.
"Mind your own business," replied Ted rudely.
"It's Ted Thomas," Clarissa told him.
"Shut up Clarissa," Ted told her, "Whose side are you on?"
"Sorry," apologised Clarissa.
"None of my business is it?" asked the man
"No it isn't," answered back Ted.
"Do you know who I am?" he asked.
"A bad tempered old so and so," thought Ted but didn't say so.

At this point, the manager broke into the conversation.

"This gentleman is a very good friend of mine" he told Ted.
"That's your bad luck, mate," thought Ted, but again had the sense not to say it.
"And perhaps before you say anything else you may regret," the manager continued, "I'd better tell you who he is."

Ted didn't care who the man was but what the manager said next made him change his mind.

"This gentleman is my good friend police sergeant Tommy Price."

At this point, Ted panicked. He looked at the other two and made a dive for the door. He was through it and out of the office, heading for the street before anyone realised what had happened. Paul and Clarissa looked at each other.

He didn't mean to do it," she told them.

With that comment, the two of them also dashed out of the office. By the time they got outside the cinema, Ted was halfway down the street and still running. They chased after him and caught up with him at the traffic lights in the centre of the town.

"Why does everything have to happen to me?" he groaned.
"You might end up with a criminal record," Paul warned him.
"I won't, will I?" asked a worried Ted.
"You can't go around assaulting police officers; they don't like it." said Paul.
"I didn't actually hit him," pointed out Ted.
"Just showered him with orange squash," chirped

up Clarissa.

"Don't remind me," groaned Ted.

"I hope he doesn't come after us," said Paul, glancing back down the street.

"Good job he doesn't know us or know where we live." said Ted.

"Clarissa did tell him your name," Paul reminded him.

"Yes," said Ted, glaring at his cousin, "That was a great help."

"I'm sorry," she apologised, "I didn't mean to cause any trouble."

"I'm just thankful he didn't get round to asking us where we lived, or you might have told him that as well," he told her.

"Do you think he'll try to find you?" asked Paul.

"He won't be able to trace me from just my name, will he?" said Ted, hopefully.

"I shouldn't think so," said Paul, trying to reassure his brother.

"What are we going to do now?" asked Clarissa

"Let's get back to the smithfield," suggested Ted. "The sooner we leave this town the better."

They made their way back to the smithfield, with Ted looking over his shoulder occasionally to make sure they weren't being followed. He nearly had a heart attack when a police car raced towards them with its siren blaring and blue lights flashing. He breathed a huge sigh of relief as it sped past them without stopping.

When they arrived at the smithfield, it took them a little time to find Uncle Idwal. Eventually they found him talking with Mervyn and some other farmers discussing the price of pigs.

"Have you had a good time?" he asked them as they approached.
"Yes thank you," they replied, trying to sound as if they meant it.
"Fantastic," thought Ted to himself, "If you call nearly getting arrested having a good time."
"Are you ready to go back to the farm or would you like to spend some more time in town?" he asked them.
"We're definitely ready to go back to the farm," Ted told him.

Uncle Idwal led the way back to where the lorry had been parked with the children following a little way behind him.

"Perhaps we should travel in the back of the lorry," suggested Ted.
"Why should we do that?" asked Paul.

"So sergeant Price won't spot us when we leave town," Ted explained.
"I hardly think they will have set up roadblocks to try and catch you," replied hid brother.
"Knowing my luck," said Ted gloomily, "they will have."
"I don't think dad would let us travel in the back of the lorry," Clarissa told them.

They arrived back at the lorry, and they all climbed into the front cab. This time, Ted had Clarissa on his lap and Paul had Sidney on his. As they drove out of the smithfield, instead of turning right as Clarissa expected her father to do, he turned left.

"Where are we going dad," she asked him
"I've got to pick something up from the station," he told her.
"It's not near the cinema is it?" asked Ted, beginning to panic.
"Nowhere near it," replied his uncle. "Why?"
"No reason," said Ted as the lorry drove on into the town.

In the centre of the town they had to stop at the traffic lights.
While they waited for them to change to green,

the children kept watch for a possible sighting of Sergeant Price. They were very relieved when the lights did change, and the lorry turned left and headed towards the railway station.

"What have you got to pick up at the railway station?" Clarissa asked her father.
"I'm not going to the railway station; I'm going to the police station." he replied.
"WHAT!" yelled Ted, causing Clarissa to jump and Sidney to bark.
"What's the matter Ted?" chuckled his uncle, "You haven't broken the law, have you?"
"If you only knew," thought Ted, "If you only knew!"
"Do you know any of the sergeants?" Clarissa asked him.
"There's only one," he told her, old Tommy Price."
"Do you know him?" she asked her father,
"Oh, yes," he replied, "your mother and I have known Tommy for years,"
"Just my luck," thought Ted.
"What's he like, dad?," asked Clarissa.
"He's all right," he told her, " but I wouldn't like to upset him, he's got a terrible temper,"
"You don't have to tell us, we know," thought Ted.

The lorry pulled up outside the police station and Uncle Idwal turned off the engine.
"Would you like to come in with me?" he asked the children.
"No thank you," they all replied.

The children watched as he disappeared inside the police station. Five minutes went by, then another five minutes and then yet another five minutes.

"Where on earth is he?" asked Ted nervously.
"He is taking his time," agreed Paul.

Suddenly, Clarissa noticed someone coming down the street towards them. She recognised the figure of Sergeant Price immediately.

"Look!" she told her cousins, pointing at the approaching policeman.
"Oh, no! It's Tommy the Terrible," groaned Ted, using a nickname he'd just thought up for the sergeant.
"What are we going to do?" asked Paul
"Quick!" said Ted, "Everyone down on the floor."

The three children scrambled down onto the floor of the lorry cab and crouched there holding

their breath. Sidney watched them from the driver's seat wondering if this was some sort of game that he could join in with. Minutes passed but they remained where they were, afraid to risk a peep out of the window in case the sergeant was standing there.
Suddenly the door was flung open. Clarissa screamed, Sidney barked, and the boys held their breath.

"What on earth are you doing?" Uncle Idwal asked them.
"Oh, it's you, uncle," said Ted breathing a huge sigh of relief.
"Of course it's me," he replied. "Who were you expecting? And what are you all doing down there?"
"I dropped some money," Ted said, thinking quickly, "and we were trying to find it."
"And did you?" asked his uncle.
"Did we what?" Ted replied.
"Find the money you dropped"
"Oh that," said Ted. "Yes, thank you,"

Uncle Idwal climbed in, started the engine and the lorry moved away from the police station much to the children's relief. The further from the town and the nearer to the farm they got, the more the children relaxed. As they travelled along, Uncle Idwal began chuckling to himself.

"What's so funny, dad?" Clarissa asked him.
"It's not funny, really," he chuckled.
"Well why are you laughing?" she asked.
"While I was in the police station", he told her, "old Tommy Price came in." he told her. "He was in a terrible mood."
"Why was he in such a bad mood?" Ted asked innocently.
"He'd been to the cinema with his daughter and some naughty boy had tipped orange squash over him from the balcony." his uncle told him.

"Oh, dear," said Ted.
"Oh dear, is right," said his uncle. "I wouldn't like to be in that boy's shoes if Tommy catches up with him. Funny thing is," he added, "that boy was also called Ted."
"Must be lots of boys called Ted," suggested Paul
"Probably hundreds," agreed Clarissa.
"More like thousands, if you ask me," added Ted.

"The journey continued in silence for a while, the silence only being broken by the occasional chuckle from Uncle Idwal.

"And what did you get up to in town today?" he suddenly asked.
"Just wandered about," said Ted.
"We went for a walk along the canal," added Paul.
"I wonder how that boy is?" wondered Clarissa.
"I'd forgotten about him," said Ted.
"What boy are you talking about?" asked his uncle.

The children started to tell him how the boy had fallen into the canal, how they had managed to pull him out and how Ted had managed to revive him.

"Goodness me!" exclaimed Uncle Idwal, "You're heroes!"
"It was nothing," Ted said modestly.
"It certainly wasn't nothing," he contradicted Ted, "I'm proud of the three of you."

He drove the lorry into a lay-by and turned off the engine.

"What are you doing?" asked Clarissa.

"I think we should go back into town and report the incident to the police." he told them.

"No!" said Ted quickly, "I'd rather not if you don't mind."

The others agreed with Ted. The last thing they wanted to do was to go back to the police station and bump into Sergeant Price.
"If that's what you want," conceded Uncle Idwal.

They drove on to the farm and when they arrived they found Aunty Gwyneth had gone to visit her friend Marian on the neighboring farm.

"At least our backs will have a chance to recover," said Ted.

On entering the farmhouse they found food waiting for them on the kitchen table. Although Ted did not have much of an appetite he did eat some of it. While Uncle Idwal went to feed the animals, the children discussed the events of the day.

"I don't think I'll go into town again," Ted told them.
'I wonder why?" said Paul, knowing only too well the reason why.
"I'm going to stay on the farm for the rest of the time we are here." he added.

"Probably a good idea," agreed his brother.
"I do hope that boy is OK," said Clarissa.
"So do I," said Ted.

Clarissa suggested a game of Scrabble. Ted wasn't very enthusiastic. He got less and less enthusiastic as the game progressed, especially when he noticed the words Paul and Clarissa were making. Paul's included, policeman, orange, arrest, and squash, while Clarissa's included prison, price, and handcuffs. They all reminded him of what had happened to him in town. The sound of a car pulling into the farmyard stopped the game.
"Who is it?" asked Ted nervously.
"It's only Mam," said Clarissa, looking out of the window.
"That's all right then," said Ted, fearing it might have been somebody else.
"That's not all right then!" disagreed his brother.
"Why?" asked Ted,
"Because it means back breaking time," explained Paul.
"Oh, heck!" said Ted, "Time for bed?"
"Time for bed," agreed Paul.
"Goodnight Clarissa," they called as they ran for the stairs.
"Why are you going to bed?" she asked them.

"We suddenly feel very tired," Paul told her.
"Our backs are especially tired," called back Ted as they disappeared up the stairs.
"Their backs are especially tired?" repeated Clarissa with a puzzled look on her face.

They quickly undressed and dived into bed. They were not a moment too soon as they heard footsteps coming up the stairs.
"Operation Sleeping Beauty?" asked Ted.
"Operation Sleeping Beauty," agreed Paul.

They closed their eyes and pretended to be asleep as the bedroom door opened and their aunty tiptoed into the room.

"Are you asleep my lovely boys?" she whispered.

She got no answer except the sound of snoring from the boys but instead of leaving the bedroom as the boys expected her to, she tiptoed across the room towards them and much to their relief she just tucked them in and left the room.

"Thank goodness she's gone," whispered Ted.
"We'd better get to sleep in case she comes back," said Paul.

"I don't think I'm going to sleep much tonight," sighed Ted, "I'm too worried about Tommy the Terrible"

"He's probably forgotten about you by now," said Paul, trying to reassure his brother.

" I doubt it," said Ted, "Knowing my luck, he'll never forget about me. I have this awful feeling I'm going to see him again."

Chapter 6.

Trouble for Ted?

Paul dropped off to sleep quite quickly but it took Ted a lot longer. When he did eventually fall asleep, he had a very restless night. He had a nightmare where he dreamt Sergeant Price had caught him, arrested him, and locked him up in the cells. If that wasn't bad enough, there was the sound of someone hammering in his nightmare and when he asked one of the policemen what it was he was told they were building some gallows on which they would hang him the following morning.
At this point in his nightmare, the cockerel in the farmyard let out a loud 'cock-a-doodle-do. Ted shot up in bed with a scream.

"I'm too young to die," he wailed.
"Uuh, what" grunted Paul, woken up by Ted's scream. "What's the matter?"
"They're building some gallows," wailed Ted, "Tommy the Terrible is going to hang me!"
"Don't be daft," Paul told him. "You've been having a nightmare."
"Can't you hear someone hammering?" asked Ted,

Paul listened and he too could hear the hammering. He got out of bed, walked to the window, and looked out.

"That's Uncle Idwal working in the farmyard, you idiot," he told his brother.
"Thank goodness for that!' said Ted, breathing a huge sigh of relief.
"BREAKFAST!" Aunty Gwyneth's voice shrieked up the stairs from the kitchen below.

The boys quickly dressed and made their way downstairs where they had a quick wash in the sink without taps before taking their places at the table.

"Haven't you forgotten something?" their aunty asked them.
"We've had a wash," Ted told her.
"I don't mean that," she replied. "You haven't given your aunty her good morning kiss",
"How could we have forgotten." muttered Ted.
"And as I missed giving you a hug last night because you were asleep in bed when I came home, I'll give you an extra big hug this morning." she announced.
"That'll be great," said Ted, not sounding a bit enthusiastic about it.

"An extra big hug!" whispered Paul. "What does she want to do, kill us?"

Each boy in turn went up to their aunty to receive their torture. It was as bad as they expected. They could swear they heard their spines cracking as they each received their hugs.

"Our backs will never stand a week of this." groaned Paul.

"Bore da boys," Uncle Idwal greeted them as he and Clarissa joined them at the table for breakfast.
"Borrow dad, uncle," replied the boys.
"I hope he doesn't want to give us a good morning hug and kiss," whispered Ted.
"Are you going to help me with some jobs today?" he asked them.
"We don't have to go into town, do we?" asked Ted.

"No, there's plenty to do on the farm." he told them.
"In that case, you've got two willing helpers," said Ted.
"Da iawn" said Uncle Idwal.
"Pardon?" asked Ted.

"Dad's saying 'good' in Welsh," explained Clarissa
"We now know four words in Welsh," said Paul proudly, borrow dad and die yawn."
"Sounds the same as English to me," whispered his brother.
"Before you help your uncle, you can help Clarissa collect the eggs from the henhouse," their aunty informed them.
"That'll be EGGCITING,' said Paul., which set Clarissa off giggling.

Ted tried to ignore his brother who enjoyed winding him up with his terrible jokes.

"We'll have a CRACKING good time," he added, slipping in another joke to annoy his brother.
"You'd better not crack any of my eggs!' warned his aunty.
"Is it muddy in the farmyard?" asked Ted.
"Yes," admitted their uncle, "you'd better put your wellingtons on before you come out."
"And you'd better make sure you take them off before you come back in," warned their aunty, "I don't want any mud on my nice clean kitchen floor,"

Their aunty gave them a basket each in which to collect the eggs.

"Now, do you know what to do?" she asked them.
"No need to EGGSPLAIN," said Paul, "We know EGGSACTLY what to do," which set Clarissa off giggling again.

The eggs were collected and taken to the kitchen where Aunty Gwyneth started putting them into boxes. Ted and Paul went to find their uncle with Clarissa running to catch them up. They found him working on the tractor.

"What do you want us to do?" asked Paul.
"You can help with the milking," he told them.
"We couldn't do that!" gasped Ted.
"Of course you can," Clarissa told him. "Don't worry, I'll show you what to do, I've helped do the milking loads of times."

Ted was not at all convinced. He'd had enough trouble dealing with the sheep and cows were a lot bigger than sheep. The thought of getting close to one of them was more than a bit alarming. On entering the milking parlor they found the cows already in their stalls waiting to be milked and were rather surprised to hear music playing.

"Why the music?" asked Ted.

"I know why," Paul told him, with a huge grin on his face.
"I don't want to know," Ted told him, knowing his brother was going to come out with another of his so-called jokes.
"Cows like MOOOSIC," he told them, "It gets them in the MOOOOD for milking.

This set Clarissa off into fits of giggles while Ted ignored his brother. Clarissa led them over to one of the cows.

"The milk is stored in the cow's udder," she explained, pointing to it hanging down below the cow. "We attach these suction cups to the teats on the udder like this and the machine does the rest,"

The boys watched as she expertly attached the suction cups to the udder and were amazed to see the milk from the udder travelling through transparent pipes to large glass containers.

"That looked fairly easy," said Ted though he was still nervous of trying it himself.
"It wasn't so easy years ago," his uncle informed him. "Before we had milking machines we had to milk each cow by hand,"

"How on earth did you do that?" asked Paul.
"Well," began his uncle, " the person doing the milking sat on a stool close enough to reach the udder and a pail or bucket was placed under the udder to catch the milk in.
Then taking a teat in each hand they squeezed and pulled it, directing the milk that came from it into the pail."

Ted dreaded to think what might happen if he ever had to milk a cow by hand.

"You're turn to have a go," Clarissa told him.
"What!" yelled Ted, thinking she meant he had to do it by hand.

He was relieved to see her holding the suction cups for him to attach to the cow's udder. Taking them from her he nervously moved closer to the cow and attempted to attach them to the udder. His first attempt failed.

"If you can't get it to work on that cow you'd better try it on an UDDER one," Paul suggested, which set Clarissa off into more giggling.

His second attempt was successful, and he was delighted to see when it was his brother's turn that Paul had even more trouble than he did.

When all the cows had been milked they were led into the cowshed before being returned to the field.

"What's next, uncle," asked Paul
"You can clean out the cowshed," he told them.
"What do we use?" asked Paul
"Those," said their uncle pointing to two objects leaning against the wall.

They reminded the boys of what they had used to clear the snow outside their house last winter.

"Use them to push the manure and straw out of the cowshed and pile it up outside. Then use the hose pipe attached to the tap over there to hose down the floor.. Understood?"
"Yes, uncle," replied the boys "Bendigedig!" said their uncle, going back to work on the tractor.
"Who's this Ben D. Gedgig chap?" asked Ted.

"Bendigedig is Welsh for wonderful," explained Clarissa as she left them to go and help her mother pack up the eggs they had collected earlier.

"It doesn't half smell in here," said Ted holding his nose as they entered the cowshed.
"Let's get it done as quickly as possible," suggested Paul.

They set to work pushing all the manure and straw outside and piling it up at the side of the cowshed. It took them quite some time to complete the job but at last they were ready to hose down the building.

"You go and turn the water on, and I'll hose it down." said Paul.

"But I wanted to do that," protested Ted.
"Tough!" replied Paul, "I've got the hosepipe!"

Muttering to himself, Ted went over to the tap and pretended to turn it on.

"It's on." he called out to his brother, with an evil smile on his face.
"You sure?" called back Paul, "There's no water coming out of this end."
"Check down the end of it," suggested Ted. "It may be blocked."

He watched as Paul brought the hosepipe up to

his face and looked down the end of it. Then he turned on the water!

"I can't see any...." began Paul.

The next moment he really could not see anything as water suddenly shot out of the hosepipe and into his face. The shock of it combined with the force of the water knocked him clean off his feet and he landed in the pile of manure and straw they had swept out of the cowshed. Ted just fell about, helpless with laughter.

"I'll kill him!' growled Paul, "I'll assassinate him!"
"Funny place to have a sit down," Ted told him.
"I'll get you for this," Paul threatened him.
"Temper, temper," said Ted, "Where's your sense of humour?"

At that moment, Paul did not have a sense of humour, only a sense for revenge!

"It's not funny!' he told his brother.
"It is from where I'm standing, chuckled Ted.
"I'm going to have to go and change and clean up," complained Paul.
"I'm sorry," apologised Ted, "I remembered how

we did the same thing to the council workmen when they were trying to get into Sleepy Hollow".

Paul stormed off across the farmyard heading for the house and Ted began to hose down the cowshed. As he was working, he heard a car pulling into the farmyard, but he ignored it and continued working. He was surprised when a minute later Paul came rushing back.

"That was a quick clean up," he told him.
"I haven't had a clean up," replied Paul. "A car has just arrived."
"I heard it," said Ted.
"It's a white one," Paul told him."
"I don't know anyone with a white car," said Ted.
"I think you do," disagreed Paul. "let me give you a few clues. This car has some writing on the side of it," Paul told him.
"Doesn't ring a bell," said Ted.
"It doesn't ring a bell," said Paul, "but it does have a siren and it's got pretty blue lights on the roof."

For a moment Ted froze and turned a deathly white and then he began to laugh.

"Nice try Paul, you nearly had me believing you!"

he told his brother.
"I'm telling you the truth," Paul insisted.
"You're just trying to get your own back for me soaking you with the hose." Ted told him.
"I only wish I was," said Paul. "If you don't believe me, come and look for yourself."

They both walked to the door and looked out into the yard. Ted felt sick. Paul had not been lying, parked in the farmyard was a police car. Uncle Idwal was talking to the driver who was still sitting in the car.

"Perhaps it's nothing to do with us," said Ted hopefully.

Neither of the boys really believed that, and when Sergeant Price stepped out of the car, Ted's worst fears were confirmed.

"It's Tommy the Terrible!" he groaned, "He's come to get me!"

"What are we going to do?" asked Paul.
"I could make a run for it," suggested Ted.
"He'd only come after you," Paul told him.
"I wish I could hear what they're saying," said Ted.
"Now's your chance," said Paul, "They're heading

this way."
"Help!" squawked Ted.
"Ted, Paul," called out Uncle Idwal, "There's someone here to see you."
"I don't want to see him," thought Ted.
"We'd better go and get it over with," said Paul.

The two boys walked slowly out of the cowshed.

"I'm very sorry about the orange squash," apologised Ted as he walked towards Sergeant Price. " It was an accident, honest. I didn't do it on purpose.
"He's telling the truth," said Paul, backing up his brother.
"Oh, it's you, is it?" said the sergeant. "Fancy it being you. This is a turn up for the book!"
"What's he on about," whispered Ted.
"Please don't arrest him," begged Paul.
"Sergeant Price hasn't come about the incident in the cinema," Uncle Idwal told them. "He's here about a different incident."
"But I haven't done anything else," protested Ted.
"Oh yes you have, young man," said the sergeant, "and we have witnesses to prove it."
"They're lying," shouted Ted. "I've been framed!"
"We have all the evidence we need," the sergeant told him.

"But…." began Ted.
"Let me finish," interrupted the sergeant. "If you want a solicitor you can phone for one later."

He winked at Uncle Idwal, took out his notebook, opened it and began to read from it.
"Yesterday afternoon at about one o'clock, you, your brother and cousin were seen walking along the canal towpath. Is that correct?"

The boys nodded and Sergeant Price continued to read from his notebook.

"A young boy was fishing and fell into the canal and would have drowned had you not pulled him out. Is that correct?" asked the sergeant.

The boys nodded again.

"In fact," continued the sergeant, "not only did you rescue him from the canal you revived him when he stopped breathing."
"Is that why you've come?" asked Ted.
"What other reason could there be?" asked the sergeant smiling.
"I thought you were going to arrest me," said Ted.
"Certainly not," said the sergeant, "I've come to thank you for saving that boy's life. That boy was

my son Martyn and if it wasn't for you he would be dead instead of recovering in hospital."

The sergeant took both of Ted's hands in his and shook them.
Aunty Gwyneth and Clarissa came out of the farmhouse to see what was going on.

Clarissa, seeing Sergeant Price holding onto both Ted's hands thought he had handcuffed him and was arresting him. She raced across the farmyard and before anyone could stop her, she delivered one of her kung-fu blows into the sergeant's stomach. He went reeling backwards and collapsed on the yard.

"Quick!" Clarissa yelled to her cousin, "Escape while you can!"

There was uproar in the farmyard. While Uncle Idwal,Ted and Paul rushed to help Sergeant Price, Aunty Gwyneth began shouting at Clarissa demanding to know what she was playing at.

"Are you all right, Tommy?" asked Uncle Idwal as they helped the Sergeant to his feet.
"I think so," he puffed.
"Oh, dear," said Clarissa, "What have I done? I'm

very sorry," she apologised.
"So you should be," wheezed the sergeant, "assaulting a police officer is a very serious offence."
"Will I have to go to prison?" she asked.
"I'll make a deal with you," said the policeman, "If your mother makes me a nice cup of tea, we'll forget about the incident."

Well of course, Aunty Gwyneth did make him a cup of tea and Clarissa did not have to go to prison. After several cups of tea and a couple of slices of Aunty Gwyneth's chocolate cake, the sergeant stood up to leave.

"Time I was getting back on duty," he told them.

They all followed him out into the yard to see him off. As he was driving away, another car pulled into the farmyard.

"I recognise that car," said Ted, "It's dad's."
"What are you doing here?" Paul asked his father as he got out of the car.
"I've come to take you home," he told his sons.
"Aren't we staying the full week?" Ted asked.
"I'm afraid not." replied his father, "something has happened which means you have to come home

straight away."
"Is Mam alright," asked Paul anxiously.
"Of course," his father reassured them. "You'd better go and pack your things while I explain things to your aunty and uncle.
"I'll give you a hand," offered Clarissa, and they went inside leaving the adults talking in the yard.

"I wonder what's going on," said Ted as they packed their cases.
"I'm sorry you're going," Clarissa told them.
"So are we," said Paul.

When they'd finished packing they made their way outside where the adults were waiting. Their father loaded the cases into the car while the boys said their goodbyes.

"Thank you for having us," said Ted.
"It's been a pleasure," their aunty told them. "You must come again for a longer visit," she told them.

The boys turned and made their way back to the car. They almost made it but not quite.

"Haven't you forgotten something?" she screeched after them.

By now, the boys knew exactly what their aunty meant. They had hoped she might have forgotten but no such luck. They turned and walked back towards her to receive the final kiss and crush.

"Goodbye, my lovely boys," she said, beginning to cry.

She grabbed Ted first and after he had suffered, Paul received the same treatment.

"I don't know why she's crying," groaned Ted as they staggered back to the car. "We're the ones in pain!"
"I don't think it's such a good idea coming back for a longer holiday, I don't think our backs could stand the strain." said Paul.
They sat in the car while their father said his goodbye to their aunty and uncle.
"She doesn't give dad a hug," observed Paul.
"Lucky old him," replied Ted.

Mr. Thomas got in the car and drove out of the farmyard, the boys waving as they went.

"Why are we coming home earlier than planned?" Ted asked his father.

"I'll tell you when we get home," he told them.

On the long journey back to South Wales they tried a number of times to get their father to explain the reason for their early return but each time he refused.

Preview of book 4

Ted and Paul - Woodland Park Boarding School.

Chapter 1

Ted and Paul's holiday in North Wales had come to a sudden end when their father had turned up unexpectedly to take them home. On the journey back to South Wales he had continually refused to tell them why they were going home early. When they arrived home, he went to put the car in the garage and the boys hurried into the house hoping they would have more success questioning their mother.

"Why have we had to come back early?" asked Ted as they walked into the kitchen.
"Didn't your father tell you?" she asked them.
"He hasn't told us anything." complained Paul. "What's the big secret?"
"I think it would be better if he told you." she replied.
"He could have done that hours ago on the journey home," muttered Ted.

Their father came into the kitchen and sat at the table.

"I expect you're wondering what's going on?" He said to his sons.
"You could say that" replied Ted. "What exactly is going on?"
"Sit down the both of you," said their father.
"I don't like this," Paul whispered to his brother as they both sat at the table. "This is not going to be good news."
"I've got some good news and bad news to tell you," he told them.
"At least it's not bad news and worse news," whispered Paul.

The boys sat silently, dreading what the bad news was going to be.

"First, the good news," announced their father.
"I've been promoted at work."
"That is good news," agreed Paul.
"Does that mean we can have extra pocket money?" asked Ted.
"Trust you to think of that!" said his father.
"Well does it?" asked Ted, determined to get an answer.
"I might be able to give you an extra 10p a week." he replied.
"Big deal!" said Ted.
"I'm sure you'll get a bit more than that," smiled

his father, "but that's not important."
"It is to us," Paul contradicted him.
"What's the bad news?" asked Ted, almost afraid to ask.
"The promotion means I'll have to travel abroad," his father told them.
"What's bad about that?" asked Paul.
"I'll have to take your mother with me," explained their father.
"Oh, that is bad news for you," joked Ted.
"You cheeky monkey!" said his mother, clipping him round the ear.
"Only joking, Mam," said Ted, rubbing his ear.
"It presents us with a problem," his father told them.
"I can't see any problem," Paul told him.
"I don't think I can accept this promotion," he told them.
"Are you mad!" said Ted, "You can't turn down a chance like this and besides we need the extra pocket money!"
"I still can't see the problem," said Paul.
"Nor me," said Ted. "Dad, you've got to take the job!"
"I'm glad you said that son." said his father, "That makes it easier for me to make my decision."
"That's settled then," said Ted.
"I still can't see the problem, " persisted Paul.

"The problem is," said their father, "What are we going to do with you two while we are away."

The boys sat in stunned silence. They assumed they would have been going with their parents. They could now see what the problem was that was so worrying their parents. They looked at each other while their parents anxiously waited for a response from their sons. Ted was first to speak.

"I thought we would be coming with you," he announced.
"If that were possible, we wouldn't have a problem," said his father, "but unfortunately we can't take you with us."

The boys felt very disappointed. It would have been great to travel abroad visiting different countries with their parents. What could they do? They didn't like the idea of not going with their parents but neither did they want to do anything to prevent their father taking the promotion. After several minutes of silence, Ted had one of his brilliant ideas.

"I've solved the problem!" he announced.

"Oh, have you?" said his father. "I can't wait to hear your solution to the problem!"

Comments from former pupils & residents of Cwmcarn village when they found out Ted and Paul stories were finally going to be published.

Lauren Barraby

I will very eagerly read these stories to my children. I know they will sit there with the same enjoyment and awe that I and many other hundreds of students have previously done.

Lisa Marie

Great fond childhood memories of Ted and Paul that will always stick with me . I would rush to get to Mr. Godwin's class for the best part of the day. Gripping adventures of Ted and Paul. I'm so pleased these stories are being published. Can't wait to share these amazing stories with my next generation, my beautiful children.

Claire Louise Morris

Mr. Godwin was a wonderful teacher and role model for me. The Ted and Paul stories were the highlight of the day. So wonderful that the stories are finally being published and I cannot wait to read them to my grandchildren.

Beki Hodges

My children still have the most amazing memories of Mr. Keith Godwin and his Ted and Paul stories and how he held the class in the palm of his hand by the way he taught and the way he wrote. I'm so grateful that their own children/our grandchildren will now be able to treasure these stories too.

Steve Phillips

Loved these stories circa 1976. Well done Keith!

Lesley Allen

I can look back over the years and remember most of my teachers, but if I was asked which lessons, I remember then it would be Mr. Godwin's. If I was asked which teacher inspired me, it would be Mr. Godwin. The most enjoyable class? Mr. Godwin's. The excitement of a Ted & Paul story and the amazing way it was read out. The silence in the classroom as we listened to every single word, not wanting it to end. Truly unforgettable! Can't wait to get to read them again.

Louise Cobb

Ted & Paul was the only book that would take me away from "Where's Wally" from the book corner. Can't wait to read this to my little girl and for my own enjoyment.

Helen Williams

Keith Godwin was an amazing and inspiring teacher loved Ted and Paul but used to dread Friday morning with the 10 questions and the homework OMG the cryptic questions for extra points had my parents baffled.

Daniel Preece

I never actually made it to Mr. Godwin's class, but I got to know him really well, when I would wait for my sister Lucy who was in his class (Lucy Preece), I would usually end up getting in some kinda trouble. He had a fantastic way of telling you off. Not only did you get told what you did wrong, but he would tell you why and how you did it. I never got the impression he was mad with me really, just disappointed with my lack of imagination. I used to have to do sewing patterns while waiting to keep me out of trouble. I still remember how to sew to this day!

Lucy Harris

Mr. Godwin was my favourite teacher, I loved his lessons and stories. Just a lovely man and being his student was an honour.

Rhys David Glyn Prosser

I was in Mrs. Hawkins class, but I remember his stories from the times the two classes were combined in the school hall.

Sarah Wilkinson

I loved the Ted and Paul stories to they were the best stories. Mr. Godwin.

Julia Barnes

Mr. Godwin was such an inspirational teacher, his Ted and Paul stories were the highlight of our day, the time when everyone in the class was in total silence. Such amazing stories which gave us all amazing memories of our time in primary school. Can't wait to read them again.

Cathy Anne Reese

Ted & Paul kept a lively class quiet each afternoon. Glad Mr. G is finally doing what we urged him to do 43 years ago! Well done.

Donna Peters

I remember my boys coming home from school. And telling me about their day. And about story time with Mr. Godwin. I look forward to my grandson reading the same stories.

Simon Davies

The best stories written by the best teacher which bring back the best memories.

Gavin Oliver

Ted and Paul was everything we went to school for it was that end of day bedtime story that we waited all day for. I'll never forget the stories of such a talented writer/teacher. Our education really stemmed from such inspirations in this school that i wish i could go back and redo my childhood.

Lauren Jarrett

I absolutely loved Mr. Godwin's classes, they were always great fun, and the Ted and Paul story he would make up for year 6 class leaving. I'd have loved a copy, wishing you the best.

Printed in Great Britain
by Amazon